187.

o all the Community.
Reminder of where I
was for the last year!
Thank you for all the letters
Best wishes!
Mairéad

Amerika Sāmoa

So'o le fau ma le fau
To tie together two pieces of fau
Proverb: To pursue a goal with united strength.

Amerika Sāmoa

An Anthropological Photo Essay

Frederic Koehler Sutter

UNIVERSITY OF HAWAII PRESS

HONOLULU

Library of Congress Catalog Card Number 84-51832
ISBN 0-8248-0990-4
Design - Frederic Koehler Sutter Ph.D.,
and Alan Whistler
Origination and separations by Quadrascan N.Z.
Bound by The New Zealand Government Printing Office.

89 88 87 86 85 84   4 3 2 1

Dedicated to the people of American Samoa

my wife Sharon

my daughter Lisenga

and to my parents Eleanor and Carl

Contents

Foreword

The Government of American Samoa decided to commission this anthropological photo essay for several reasons: to create a pictorial record of our culture for future generations; to enable overseas Samoans to stay in touch with their heritage; to introduce our islands and culture to those who wish to know more about American Samoa.

Although a great deal of effort often goes into the conservation of natural resources, it is unfortunate that culture and geographic beauty are seldom defined as such resources. We in American Samoa are keenly aware that God's gift to us is the incredible beauty of our islands and our way of life, our culture. This anthropological photo essay records that heritage for future generations.

Today many of our people are able to take advantage of opportunities to further their education and employment overseas. American Samoans are found all over the U.S. mainland and in many foreign lands as well. Some have been away a long time; others were born far from home. For those who were born in Samoa, this book will evoke memories of their childhood: the smell of the umu, the sounds of the kava ceremony, the joys of White Sunday. And for those who have never been in Samoa, the book will provide visual images to reinforce the stories that are told, as well as their family pride in being American Samoan.

To those who wish to learn more about American Samoa and its culture, these photographs and the accompanying proverbial expressions will provide intimate glimpses of the daily and seasonal activities that make up the Samoan way of life, thereby contributing to an understanding of what it is like to be Samoan.

The Government of American Samoa chose Dr Sutter to produce this book because of his previous work *Samoa: A Photographic Essay*. As you will see in the following pages, he combines the skill of the expert photographer with the perception and sensitivity of the field anthropologist to capture peak moments of our culture.

It gives me great pleasure to present *Amerika Sāmoa: An Anthropological Photo Essay*, a book that successfully records both the beauty of our islands and the richness of our culture.

Peter Tali Coleman
Governor of American Samoa

Preface

Cultural awareness, time, patience, and co-operation are all necessary for producing an anthropological photo essay.

Foremost among these requirements is an awareness of the cultural spectrum. This includes the ability not just to recognize the primary colors of life's daily activities, but also to know the subtle shades revealed in a people's celebrations and ceremonies, and the milestones that mark their lives.

It is one thing to be aware of all this but quite another to locate and be allowed to record the behaviors and events that illustrate the culture. To achieve this, time, lots of time, is required. The minimum is a year. Some activities follow a daily pattern, but others occur once a week, once a year, or even less frequently.

In Samoa, each day begins with cleaning up the family compound. People go about their lives, attending school, working in offices, planting and harvesting the land, and collecting the resources of the sea. In the afternoon, there is time to relax and play before the family gathers for evening prayer. Every Saturday, preparations are made for Sunday's communal meal, and once a year, the legislature opens, Children's Sunday is celebrated, and the *palolo* are netted.

Periodically the daily round is punctuated by special occasions, called *fa'alavelave*, which underscore the basic rhythm of family and village life. Events such as the bestowal of a title, a tattooing, or the dedication of a church are awaited, not scheduled at predictable intervals. Perhaps once in five years, a *lagi soifua* occurs — a funeral held while the individual still lives and can enjoy the fine mats, food, and speeches given in his or her honor.

To record all this photographically requires the co-operation and assistance of the participants. It requires a people who are proud of their culture, understanding, and generous enough to share their way of life.

American Samoa's most precious resource is not a new technology or industrial product, but its culture. With the advance of industrialized society, the demands of a wage economy, and the cultural homogenization that is encouraged by rapid transportation and communication, many unique and irreplaceable cultural practices have become diluted. This anthropological photo essay is an attempt to record traditional practices by documenting the rich and varied celebration of the human spirit that is every Samoan's heritage.

The book is divided into eight sections. The Prologue is based on the creation myth as told in Manu'a, the easternmost islands. This is followed by a traditional view of activities associated with Dawn and the Day. Pago Pago and Beyond addresses some aspects of modern life as well as American Samoa's involvement with the Pacific community. Milestones is an anthology of events that mark important junctures in a Samoan's life. These events reflect the culture's vitality and values just as the proverbs cited are a distillation of its wisdom. The section on Religion portrays American Samoa's spiritual life and heritage. Close of Day is devoted to activities associated with the end of work and a time of relaxation and recreation. The Epilogue presents a final look at a group of beautiful islands and their people.

An undertaking of this magnitude could not succeed without the assistance, support, and encouragement of many people. First and foremost, I would like to thank Governor Peter Tali Coleman for his enthusiastic support. I especially wish to express my gratitude to Director of Economic and Development Planning Joseph Pereira, whose foresight and vision made the project possible.

Over the past two years, many people have generously given of themselves, their knowledge, hospitality, and services. Lieutenant Governor Tufele Li'a and High Chief Fuimaono have responded to every request for assistance. Governor's Special Assistant Palauni Tuiasosopo not only helped remove many an obstacle but also provided personal friendship, as did Eni Hunkin and Failautusi Avegalio.

Moving about the islands was a major consideration. On Tutuila, several young men carried the equipment and at times assisted me in getting up and down mountainsides. My thanks to Mu and Nofo Mafatau, Tupuga Leota, and Anetone Fuga. On Swains Island, nine-year-old Samoa Fio was my guide and assistant. For more than a year, Alo and Marilyn Anesi and Jack and Mary Pavitt of Pavitt's U-Drive provided the ultimate in co-operation.

At sea, Captain Nick Marinkovich put his boat the *Elspeth* and its helicopter at my disposal. Without his generous help, several photographs could not have been taken.

Throughout the project, South Pacific Island Airways gave every possible assistance. I wish especially to thank the president of the airline, George Wray, for his total commitment to the project, which was reflected in the support given by his staff. In Honolulu, assistance was provided by Pita Salā, inflight by Nafanua Pātū and Tevita Prescott, and in American Samoa, by Chuck Phelan, Evelyn Tuia, and Captains Kaher, Dow, and Paul.

Even with the abundance of hospitality accorded a stranger in Samoa, there are times when one longs for the intimate warmth of an old and deep friendship. On Tutuila, this was given by Rob and Loma Shaffer, Va'a and Julie Afoa, Eti and Telia Sa'aga, Rev. Elia and Galoane Ta'ase, and Puleisili and Mereane Tuiolosega. In Manu'a, Leuta Faleafine, Bert and Joan Marian, and Rev. Salesa and his family always provided hospitality and warm friendship.

My deepest gratitude goes to my assistant Herman Tuiolosega for his insights and suggestions. Although burned by the sun and drenched by the rain, he always maintained his sense of humor and dedication to the project.

Without the help of all these people, the project could not have succeeded.

Thank you all.
Thank you Samoa.

FKS
Fogāgogo, Tutuila

Amerika Sāmoa

Prologue — the Creation

"Tagaloa ... the god who made all things ...
traversed the illimitable void."

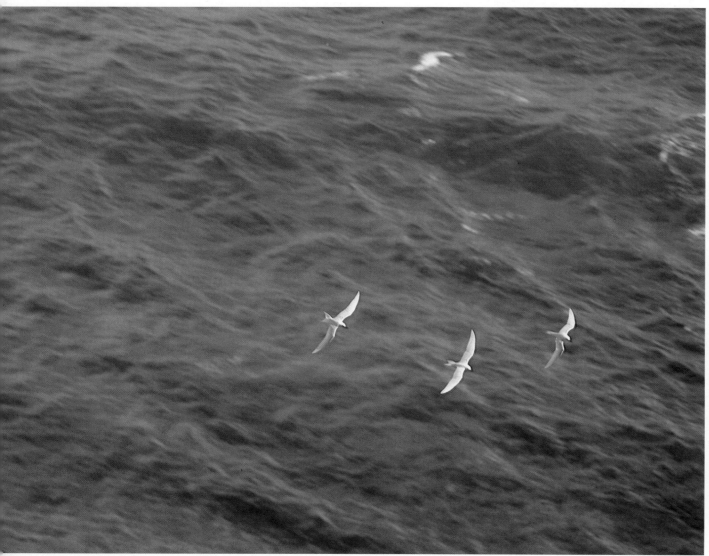

"He assumed the form of the Tulī and went about to visit the lands; but no lands could be seen, only the wide expanse of waters."

"At a point at which he took his stand, up sprang a rock."

"Tagaloa said to the rock divide! and the heaven was born ... and Immensity and Space, and the palm of clouds ... and commencing where the Eastern Group (Manu'a) now stands he caused it to emerge ..."

and Swains

and Rose.

"The creator looked down and Tutuila (and 'Aunu'u) emerged."

'Then said Tagaloa to the heaven-raising king,
'Come and raise the heavens' … He went and
brought the first of all vegetable growths and with
these he succeeded in raising the heavens."

"Then he stood on the tops of the mountains and
trod them down so as to prepare them well for …
habitation."

"And hither came from heaven the peopling vine
..."

"… which gave to Tutuila its inhabitants."

"That they may Tagaloa entertain."

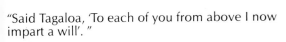
"Said Tagaloa, 'To each of you from above I now impart a will'."

"Your faces they must shine, I so ordain."

13

Ua sanisani fa'amanuao.
The joy of the welcome is like the birds greeting the
dawn. *Proverb.*

The Dawn

From Swains to Tutuila the day begins.

'E ā le puga nisi, ā le 'ana nisi.
Let each do a fair share of the work. *Proverb.*

Na o le taeao o faiva.
One should go fishing (hunting) only in the
morning.
Proverb: Early morning is the best time for work.

"They are a very cleanly people, both about their houses, their persons, and their food. They bathe at least twice a day." (Williams)

"Every morning at daylight every particle, weed, fallen leaf, and rubbish is carefully picked up." (Williams)

Youth scraping medicinal bark for his grandfather's morning tea.

Ta te gase a uluga.
Let us die together.
Proverb: Late for school.

Lutia i Puava 'ae mapu i Fagalele
Distressed at Puava but we shall rest at Fagalele
Proverb: Better things are coming

Fine mats are hung out to air in the morning sun.

The people go about their daily lives — on wings, on foot, on wheels.

E tu manu, 'ae le tu logologo.
The town crier is reliable, a rumor suspect. *Proverb.*

"[Issues] were argued on both sides with a calmness that seldom characterizes debate in more civilized countries and with an acuteness that does credit to their senses." (Williams)

23

Po'o ua atoatoa ea tupe i le fala?
Are all the discs on the mat?
Proverb: Are all present?

The Day

Fa'aafu fa'aufi.
Search for the wild yam.
*Proverb: Find the 'i'e 'i'e vine and follow it to the
source. Solve the problem.*

Ua vela le fala.
The mat is warm.
*Proverb. Applied to any performance that takes a
long time.*

Ua numi le fau.
It's more complicated than it looks. *Proverb.*

Ua o gatasi le futia ma le umele.
We must be of one mind in this undertaking.
Proverb.

Ua api le ulu.
The mark is near.
Proverb: The end is in sight.

So'o le fau.
To tie together two pieces of *fau*.
Proverb: To pursue a goal with united effort.

Na si'i le faiva o se alili, a ua maua ai le puiali'i.
They were searching for shellfish but found much
more. *Proverb.*

Fa'atauga 'o'a.
Like the pressing out of the *'o'a*.
Proverb: Slowly and thoroughly.

Ia ifo le fuiniu i le lapalapa.
May the cluster of nuts bow to the midrib of the
leaf.
Proverb: The individual is responsible to the family.

Mountain plantations.

Se'i totō le ta'amu te'evao.
Plant the giant taro to control the weeds. *Proverb.*

O le aso ma le filiga'afa, o le aso ma le mata'inatila.
Sennit should be made daily, and daily the rigging must be examined.
Proverb: Act only after mature reflection.

Ua se fau e ta'i.
Like the twisting of a cord.
Proverb: A unanimous decision.

Fa'asavali a nunu.
Like the return from the *nunu*.
Proverb: Patiently and thoroughly done.

Ua tatā lali lapopoʻa.
Beat the big drums.
Proverb: Such a problem requires the experience of a chief.

Ua osofia moega luaga.
The purlins are well joined.
Proverb. Referring to a decision that follows tradition.

36

Mālo le onosa'i.
Congratulations to patience. *Adage.*

Ua tu'u i tai le va'a tele.
The big net has been spread.
Proverb: Listen and consider the orator's words.

O le seuseu ma le fata.
Fish with a proper net.
Proverb: Do it the right way.

38

Ua suluia le pagi.
The bait has been lit up [by the rising sun].
Proverb. Applied to secrets divulged.

O le sapatu moe 'ese.
The barracuda that sleeps apart.
Proverb. Praise for a person's strength and skill.

Fili e le tai se agava'a.
Let the sea determine the quality of the boat.
Proverb.

E ala i aso.
Some days one is lucky. *Proverb.*

Dawn, and the town awakens.

O le sau o le ola.
Life-giving dew.
Proverb. An expression of gratitude.

Pago Pago and Beyond

Talanoa atu, 'ae le talanoa manu.
The bonitos swim about thoughtlessly but the
seagulls are on the alert.
Proverb: Woe to the incautious.

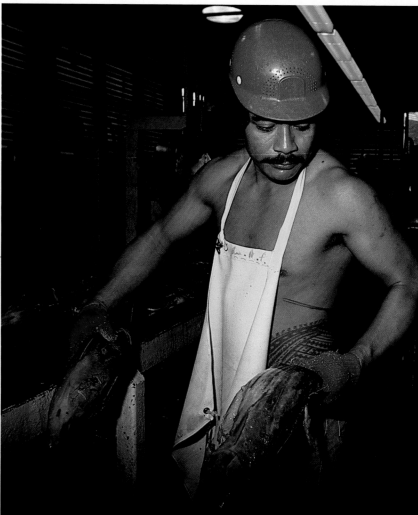

Ua leai se ulu e ala.
There is not even time to scratch one's head.
Proverb. Referring to work that keeps one's hands busy.

"They appeared very knowing merchants ... lively with all, which is indeed their natural disposition." (Williams and Barff)

Ua tofo i tino matagi lelei.
A favorable wind is felt on the body.
Proverb. Referring to the joy of expectation.

Ua iloa i va'a lelea.
Seen as briefly as voyagers carried away by the wind.
Proverb. Friendly reproof for too short a visit.

Sa matou tu'u la'au mai nei.
On our journey we have enjoyed much hospitality.
Proverb.

Ia 'oso 'ati'ati.
Dig out even the small pieces [of yam].
Proverb: Be frugal.

Aua ne'i galo Afi'a i lona vao.
Let not Afi'a be forgotten in his forest.
Proverb: Remember those left behind

E o'u le asō, 'ae o oe taeao.
Today my turn, tomorrow yours. *Proverb.*

"Men, women, and children are allowed to speak and give their opinions ... " (Williams)

"Upon the whole the government may be said to be a popular one for all important ... determinations are come to by a meeting of the whole of the people with the chief at the head." (Williams)

Each island nation's anthem is sung in its native tongue.

Ua fuifui fa'atasi, 'ae vao 'ese'ese.
Gathered into one flock from different parts of the forest. *Proverb.*

Heads of state and delegates arrive for the South Pacific Conference.

Ua malie ma le faga i Pa'au.
We are satisfied with the reception at the bay of Pa'au. *Proverb.*

A papal delegate and Samoa's cardinal preside over the formation of the new Diocese of Pago Pago.

American Samoa helps Western Samoa celebrate its independence day.

The American Samoa Arts Council performs at the inauguration of the governor of Hawaii.

The opening of the South Pacific Games.

O le ti'a ulu tonu lou finagalo.
Your will is like a *ti'a* that flies to its goal.
Proverb. Expression of courtesy and respect.

O le ua na fua mai Manu'a.
A rain that originated in Manu'a. *Proverb.* Said of an event for which due notice was given.

The women's golf team wins the gold.

E manatua pule, 'ae le manatua fa'alaeo.
Proverb: Compassion is remembered, destruction forgotten.

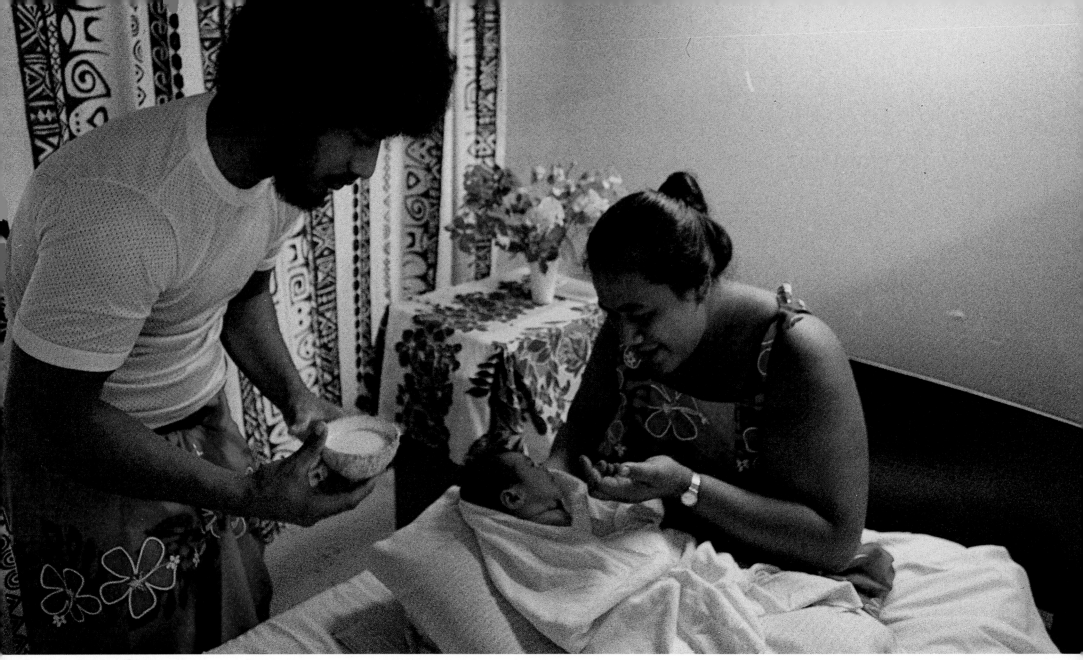

E tasi, 'ae afe.
Only one, but worth a thousand. *Proverb.*

A boy's first haircut.
E valavala a tumanu.
The shagginess of a young banana bunch.
Proverb applied to that which will mature well.

Milestones

The hair is added to the family's ceremonial headress.

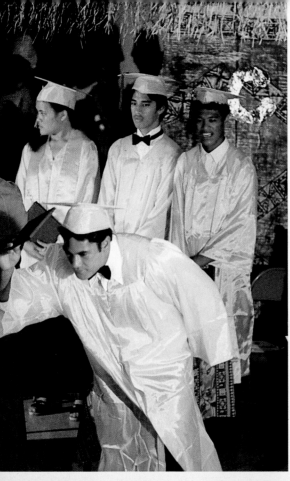

Ua tino le soifua, ua to i tua Apolima.
Life is assured, Apolima has been passed.
Proverb. A danger has been avoided.

Induction into the Army.
Tau ina ta ma fa'apio.
May it end with threats, but not come to blows.

Ia manuia le malaga.
Blessings on your journey. *Adage.*

The groom's relatives contribute money.

A wedding exchange: The bride's family presents
fine mats.

Ua le sula fala o 'Ie'ie.
'Ie'ie's mats were not acknowledged.
Proverb: Expression of joy for such abundance that
there isn't strength enough to thank for everything.

The extended family prepares to bestow its title.

Each branch of the family makes its presentation.

O le vaivai o le fe'e.
The softness of an octopus.
Proverb. A calm but momentous speech.

A careful record is kept.
Avatu ni lo, aumai ni lo.
Proverb: Tit for tat.

Sāō faʻalālelei!
Thank you, it is very beautiful.
Expression used to acknowledge a fine mat.

Celebrating the new title.

"The Chief held one end of the cloth … in his hands leaving the other to drag after him … and presented it in a rather stately manner." (Williams and Barff)

E sua le 'ava, 'ae to le 'ata.
The kava plant is dug up, but a twig is planted immediately.
Proverb: The family is immortal.

Ua lauiloa e pili ma sē.
It is known by every lizard and grasshopper.
Proverb.

The title is bestowed.

Celebation of a *lagi soifua*, a funeral held while the
guest of honor still lives and can enjoy the food, fine
mats, and speeches.

Ia e vae o Vaeau.
May your legs be like Vaeau's.
Proverb: Hurry!

Sili le foe.
Put away the paddle.
Proverb: Time to leave the work to others.

Tuai tuai ta te ma'ona ai.
Long in coming but satisfying when it does.
Proverb. Refers to a giant ground oven.

As a girl from each family dances, friends and relatives join in and contribute money to the new church.

Fa'atoetoe le muli o le ola.
Keep the remainder of the basket for others.
Proverb: Show love and kindness to everyone.

Shadow performer.

Celebrating the 150th anniversary of the arrival of
John Williams, the first missionary.

"The name of the bay is Le One (Leone) ... in no
place have I landed where better arrangements
were made or greater order preserved." (Williams)

78

Flag Day celebrates the day the islands became American Samoa.

Se'i fono le pa'a ma ona vae.
Look before you leap. *Proverb.*

O le taeao na i Saua.
The morning that was at Saua.
Proverb. Expressing joy and appreciation of a great event.

O le va'a ua mafa tautai.
The boat is full of captains.
Proverb: There's an abundance of skill here.

80

Religion

Sunday morning — the smoke from the ground ovens rises.

O le gase a ala lalovao.
The paths in the bush never disappear.
Proverb: Traditions survive.

Sunday rest.

Ia uluulu matāfolau.
To go from house to house.
*Proverb. Analgous to the Holy Spirit going from
heart to heart.*

Children's Sunday, the traditional day for baptisms.

Ia fua le niu.
May the coconut palm bear a rich harvest.
Proverb: May you be blessed with many children.

Pastor's school — learning to read.

Evening Bible study.
O le uta a le poto e fetāla'i
A wise man thinks before speaking. *Proverb.*

O le pō.
Preparing the pastor's food for the next day.

Alofa moli pō.
Love shown at night. *Proverb.*

Choir practice.
O le va'a fau pō fau ao.
A boat is being built day and night. *Proverb.*

A death in the village.
O le pā ua sala i le maga.
The hook has been torn from the shaft. *Proverb.*

Villagers keep vigil with the family, singing hymns
throughout the night.

Ua tagi le Fatu ma le 'Ele'ele.
The stones and the earth wept. *Proverb.*

O le mamao a siu i tila.
The distance of the top of the mast.
*Proverb: When the mast is sighted, loved ones will
soon be home. An assurance of reunion after death.*

Close of Day

Ua pipili tia 'ae mamao ala
The hilltops are near, but the roads to them are
long. *Proverb*

Māmā i avega si'i.
A burden is light when first lifted. *Proverb.*

Ua tō i lologamata.
He is secure in the net.
*Proverb: Said of something done with so much skill
that success is assured.*

95

In the evening there is time to relax.
Ua fa'ala'au tū i vanu.
Like a tree standing near a precipice. *Proverb.*

E mu'a le vao.
The wood is still green.
Proverb. Apology for mistakes due to inexperience

Fa'ape'ape'a le tū.
Like the swift bird that never rests. *Proverb.*

Ua se i'a e sola.
He is like a fish that escaped.
Proverb. Simile for speed.

Ua lelea le laumea.
Dry leaves are carried away by the wind.
Proverb. Allusion to troops routed.

Ua tusa tau'au.
Both shoulders are of equal strength.
Proverb referring to well-matched partners.

Ua se vi e toli.
Like fruits shaken from the vī tree.
Proverb applied to defeated cricketers.

"Samoans are a fine race of people. The men in particular are well proportioned, some of gigantick stature." (Williams)

Even at twilight the fishermen go off.

O le malie ma le tu'u.
Every shark has its price.
Proverb: Every act receives its reward.

Palolo netting once a year.
O le upega e fili i le pō, 'ae talatala i le ao.
The net that was tangled at night will be
straightened in the morning.
Proverb: To settle a dispute.

Lighting the lanterns.

Evening prayers.

Talo lua Tuna ma Fata.
Pray for both Tuna and Fata.
Proverb: Don't restrict your love to only one person.

When guests depart, a farewell party is given.

'Oa'oa i faleseu.
Delight in the hunter's shelter.
Proverb. Inward joy.

Ua patipati ta'oto le Fe'epō.
Fe'epō clapped his hands lying down.
Proverb. Expression of joy.

E tasi le pō 'ae ogaoga.
Only one night but a long one. *Proverb.*

Late at night a family gathers to discuss plans for the morrow.

Beneath the Southern Cross, day and night meet on the horizon.

Pago Pago harbor.

Epilogue

"A village nestles in its grove of palms." (R.L. Stevenson)

Ia mālū le vai i lou finagalo.
May your mind be like cool water. *Proverb.*

O siʻufofoga.
Echo.

A'e i le Pola ne'i gasē, ne'i sosola o manu ē.
Climb the Pola noiselessly lest the game birds fly away.

Ua ta'oto le ataata o Taulelei.
The reflection of Taulelei lies on the waters
Proverb: The descendants will be handsome.

Notes

COVER. The islands of Ofu and Olosega. [Aerial off Ofu]

PAGE ii. Samoan youths proudly parade the flags of the United States and American Samoa during Flag Day. Each year American Samoa celebrates the raising of the American Flag on 17 April 1900. **So'o le fau ma le fau.** Schultz, 168. [Pago Pago, Tutuila].

Prologue – The Creation

The islands of American Samoa are situated in the South Pacific, about halfway between Australia and Hawaii. They lie some 15° south of the equator, at about 170° west. All are volcanic in origin. The five high islands have abundant rainfall and lush vegetation. The remaining two islands are atolls – rings of exposed coral resting on submerged volcanoes.

PAGE 4. *Left.* Tulī – a white seabird. [Off the coast of Ofu]
Right, Spectacular volcanic formations abut many of the islands. [Eastern end of Olosega]

PAGE 5. Ofu, Olosega, and Ta'u comprise the islands of Manu'a some 65 miles east of Tutuila. Geologically they are the oldest and socially the most traditional of the group. [Aerial off Manu'a]

PAGE 6. Tutuila, with the small island of 'Aunu'u off its coast, contains two-thirds of the territory's land and over 90 percent of the population. [Aerial off 'Aunu'u]

PAGE 7. *Left*, Mountain ranges of Tutuila. [Mt Alava, Tutuila]
Top right, Swains Island, 280 miles north of Tutuila is a perfect atoll with a central freshwater lagoon. It has been privately owned by the Jennings family since 1856. [Swains Island from the sea]
Bottom right, Rose, an uninhabited atoll 250 miles east of Tutuila, is a fish and wildlife preserve. [Aerial off Rose]

PAGE 8. The moist tropical climate supports lush vegetation. A giant banyan tree frames Mt Matafao (2,142 ft.), the highest mountain on Tutuila [Tafuna, Tutuila]

PAGE 9. *Left*, Large bird's nest ferns grow on the forest floor. [In the mountains behind Malaeloa, Tutuila]
Middle, At higher elevations wild orchids bloom beneath the canopy of the rainforest. [Mt Alava road, Tutuila]
Right, Dawn – sleeping clouds rise from the mountaintops. [Mt Matafao]

PAGES 10-13. The Samoans are members of the Polynesian race, whose ancestors migrated from island Southeast Asia some three thousand years ago. They possess their own language and customs. The traditional Samoan way, or *fa'a Sāmoa*, focuses on the extended family, or *āiga*, which may contain several related Western-style families. The head of the *āiga*, is the *matai*, or chief. Families tend to be large and are closely knit. [Samoa]

The Dawn

The morning sunburst marks the beginning of a new day. For many, a superior system of roads provides easy access to town. Throughout the islands, children leave for school. In the rural areas, the men leave for their plantations or go fishing while the sun is still low. The women take care of their households, fish in the shallows of the lagoon, or weave the precious fine mats.

PAGE 14. Dawn — the lights around Pago Pago harbor still glitter, the last clouds drift from Mt Pioa, the Rainmaker, and the workday begins. **Ua sanisani fa'amanuao.** Schultz, 131. [Pago Pago harbor, Tutuila]

PAGE 15. *Left*, On Swains Island, villagers wake as the morning sun filters through their mosquito nets. The traditional Samoan house is ideally suited to the climate. [Taulaga, Swains Island]
Right, Most villages are made up of a score or more extended families living in adjoining houses. The classic village has one or more churches, and is built around a *malae* or village green which is used for ceremonial occasions and recreation. [Vailoatai, Tutuila]

PAGE 16. *Left*, Three youths on a fishing expedition carry their family's handmade outrigger canoe down to the lagoon. **'E ā le puga nisi** ... Brother Herman, 7. [Sa'ilele, Tutuila]
Right, A young hunter armed with gun and bush knife leaves for the mountains where he will stalk pigeons, edible fruit bats, and wild pigs. **Na o le taeao o faiva.** Schultz, 530. [Masefau Tutuila]

PAGE 17. Before the sun gets too hot, a father and son leave for their plantation. There they will cultivate and weed their crops of *taro* and banana. [Olosega]

PAGE 18. *Left*, Samoans are a cleanly people and most bathe twice a day — in the morning and after work. All the islands have running water. In the outer villages people enjoy an outdoor shower.
"They are a very cleanly people ... " Williams. [Faga'itua, Tutuila]
Middle, Everyone contributes to the family's welfare. Each morning the children from toddler to teenager pick up the rubbish and fallen leaves. Most villages resemble well-groomed parks.
"Every morning at daylight ... " Williams. [Fiti'uta, Ta'ū]
Right, A young man scrapes the bark of the *toa* tree. This will be pounded and squeezed through a cloth, to produce a juice that will be mixed with water and drunk by his grandfather as a digestive aid. [Lumā, Ta'ū]

PAGE 19. Free education is available to all children of American Samoa from elementary through secondary school. Each elementary school chooses its own distinctive uniform. **Ta te gase a uluga.** Schultz, 3. [Fiti'uta, Ta ū]

PAGE 20. Traditionally, old people in Samoa are revered and cared for. They continue to contribute to the family's welfare throughout their lives. Old women in particular are respected for their knowledge of genealogy. This woman takes time to air some of the family's fine mats in the morning sun. [Nu'uuli, Tutuila]

PAGE 21. *Left*, Untitled young men, called *taulele'a*, provide society's muscle. This young man shaves the lawn with a bush knife. **Lutia i Puava ...** Brown, 196. ['Ili'ile, Tutuila]
Right, Sporting a traditional tattoo that extends from his upper pectoral muscles to below his knees, this young man enjoys the convenience of a power mower. ['Ili'ili, Tutuila]

PAGE 22. *Left*, A village mayor announces a morning work project and a meeting of the chiefs. **E tu manu ...** Schultz, 547. [Olosega]
Right, A council of chiefs, or village *fono*, meets for a discussion. Each family's chief or *matai* has an opportunity to give his or her view. Decisions are not made until a consensus is reached.
"[Issues] were argued on both sides ... " Williams. [Leone, Tutuila]

PAGE 23. *Top*, American Samoa's international airport accommodates jets from overseas as well as small propeller planes that fly between the islands. [Tafuna, Tutuila]
Bottom left, Dressed in her traditional *puletasi*, a matching tunic and sarong, this woman is on her way to visit a relative. [Olosega]
Bottom right, Father and son enjoy the cool morning air. [Le'alā, Tutuila]

The Day

American Samoa is a fascinating blend of the traditional and the modern. Elementary school children learn to count with shells while teenagers program computers. Women take time to weave mats and search the lagoon for shellfish as well as holding jobs throughout the territory. Many men not only work in town but have mastered the skills required to make a plantation, work with wood, or fish the sea.

PAGE 24. *Left*, Throughout the education system, the usual elementary and high school curricula are supplemented with courses in the Samoan language, culture, and arts.
Po'o ua atoatoa ea tupe ile fala? Brown, 113. [Faleāsao, Ta'ū]
Right, Whenever possible, indigenous materials are used in the classroom.
Fa'aafu fa'aufi. Brown, 63. [Olosega]

PAGE 25. It is a long journey from counting with fingers and shells in elementary school to working with computers in high school. [Lepuapua, Tutuila]

PAGE 26. *Left*, With skill and patience a master craftswoman supervises a child's *siapo* or tapa-cloth design. Through classroom instruction and special programs offered by the museum, school children learn the art of producing, designing, and printing *siapo*.
Ua numi le fau. Schultz, 94. [Nu'uuli, Tutuila]
Right, In the Community College, students master the intricacies of the human anatomy. [Mapusaga, Tutuila]

PAGE 27. Old women take pride in continuing to use their weaving skills. This grandmother keeps her grandchild close as she works on a mat.
Ua vela le fala. Schultz, 165. [Sa'ilele, Tutuila]

PAGE 28. *Left*, Three sisters enjoy a lively discussion while doing the family laundry.
Ua o gatasi le futia ma le umele. Brother Herman, 9. [A'umi, Tutuila]
Right, The skills are passed from one generation to the next. Using materials she herself has gathered and prepared, this woman is making a hot pad. [Fagatogo, Tutuila]

PAGE 29. *Top*, Samoans are a very social people and enjoy working together whenever possible.
Bottom, Three women from the same family share the work of weaving a very large fine mat.
Ua api le ulu. Brown, 87. [Lumā, Ta'ū]

PAGE 30. *Left*, With some guidance from the head of the household, the women of the family hang a new set of blinds.
So'o le fau. Schultz, 168. [Vaitogi, Tutuila]
Right, Women also specialize in shallow-water fishing called *figota*.
Na si'i le faiva . . . Schultz, 433. [Fatumafuti, Tutuila]

PAGE 31. *Left*, The intricate and demanding skills of making *siapo*, or tapa, are practiced and taught by this master craftswoman.
Fa'atauga 'o'a. Schultz, 163. [Vaitogi, Tutuila]
Right, The traditional skills of printing *siapo* are carried over to silk screening. [Fagatogo, Tutuila]

PAGE 32. All the high islands possess dramatic scenery. The shortage of flat land necessitates cropping on the slopes of the mountains. A suitable area of bush is cleared, and *taro* or bananas planted. [Mountains behind Afono, Tutuila]

PAGE 33. *Left*, A youth climbs a coconut palm the most useful tree in the islands. The trunk is a source of wood for fuel and posts. The leaves are woven into baskets and food trays or even used for thatch. The nut's outer husk is a ready source of fuel, and its thick fibers are treated and braided into twine. The mature nut is a source of oil, and the grated meat when squeezed produces a thick cream used in cooking.
Ia ifo le fuiniu i le lapalapa. Schultz, 177. [Ofu]
Right, Taro is staple to Samoa, as wheat is to North America and rice to Asia. The edible tuber can be baked or boiled. The severed stem is replanted, takes root and after several months produces another taro.
Se'i totō le ta'amū te'evao. Schultz, 187. [Taro garden on mountains near Pago Pago]

PAGE 34. *Left*, The fibers of the coconut husk are soaked in the sea before being pounded.
O le aso ma le filiga'afa . . . Schultz, 148. [Si'ufaga, Ta'ū]
Right, Several times a week, the men gather to work at making coconut sennit. The prepared fibers are rolled together and braided into an incredibly strong twine. **Ua se fau e ta'i.** Schultz, 167 [Si'ufaga, Ta'ū]

PAGE 35. In Manu'a, a fisherman weaves a fishtrap from the roots of the 'ie'ie vine, tying them together with coconut twine. The traps are laid in shallow waters from January through April. The small fish caught are used as live bait for deep-sea fishing.
Fa'asavali a nunu. Schultz, 266. [Olosega]

PAGE 36. *Left*, Carpenters hollow out the trunk of a tree to make a giant drum. When struck with a heavy pole, the *lali* gives forth a deep, resonant boom, calling the people to church.
Ua tatā lali lapopoʻa. Schultz, 500. [Aʻoloau, Tutuila]
Right, In no other part of the world are houses built like Samoan *fales*. Traditionally, the beams are lashed together with coconut twine; no nails are needed.
Ua osofia moega luaga. Schultz, 140. [Tafuna, Tutuila]

PAGE 37. *Left*, High in the mountains young men search a streambed for crayfish. [Stream behind Malaeloa, Tutuila]
Right, A prolonged underwater hunt is rewarded. [Stream behind Malaeloa, Tutuila]

PAGE 38. *Left*, At the entrance to Pago Pago Harbor, a group of relatives construct a communal fish trap.
O le seuseu ma le fata. Brown, 85. [Fatumafuti, Tutuila]
Right, A skilled net thrower stalks a school of fish.
Ua tuʻu i tai le vaʻa tele. Schultz, 18. [ʻAunuʻu, Tutuila]

PAGE 39. *Left*, In the shallow waters between Ofu and Olosega, a fisherman sets his trap, surrounding it with sand and coral to hold it in place.
Ua suluia le pagi. Schultz, 497. [Āsaga between Ofu and Olosega]
Right, With practiced eye and skilful arm, a spearfisherman stalks the large fish that feed among the breakers.
O le sapatu moe ʻese. Schultz, 45. [Olosega]

PAGE 40. *Left*, When a fish is sighted, a fisherman slaps the surface with his spear, noting where the fish hides. He then dives and spears it beneath a coral ledge. [Ofu]
Right, Far out at sea, the men pursue their quarry in sunshine or stormy weather.
Fili e le tai se agavaʻa. Brown, 90. [Out at sea]

PAGE 41. Sometimes one is lucky and the catch is good, very good. Wrasse (Labridae; Chelinus Undulatus Ruppell, 1835),
E ala i aso. Schultz, 509. [Out at sea]

Pago Pago and Beyond

The name Pago Pago is frequently used to refer to the entire urban settlement around the bay, which in fact is made up of three villages — Utulei, Fagatogo, and Pago Pago. Although each village in American Samoa has its own council of chiefs, this area is the seat of the central government and much of the territory's commercial life. American Samoa is very much a part of the wider Pacific and has not only hosted the South Pacific Conference and received representatives from all over the world, but also frequently sends delegations to Western Samoa and beyond.

PAGE 42. At dawn, sunlight reaches into the crater that surrounds the town area. Clockwise from left are the *Queen Salamasina*, which travels between American and Western Samoa, the dome-shaped buildings of the territorial legislature, and the white-columned court house. [Fagatogo Tutuila]

PAGE 43. *Left*, Throughout American Samoa, school buses pick up the children in the morning and bring them home at the end of each day. [Fagatogo, Tutuila]
Right, Now a store, Sadie Thompson's Mart was formerly a rooming house made famous in Somerset Maugham's short story, play, and film "Rain".
O le sau o le ola. Schultz, 468. [Fagatogo, Tutuila]

PAGE 44. *Top left*, A multimillion-dollar fishing vessel leaves Pago Pago harbor on its way to the western Pacific. Over fifty such ships make up the tuna fishing fleet.
Talanoa atu, 'ae le talanoa manu. Schultz, 42. [Pago Pago, Tutuila]
Bottom left, Each vessel is air conditioned and equipped with sonar, a satellite communication system, computers, a helicopter, and several small power launches. [Atu'u, Tutuila]
Right, The fishing fleet lands enough tuna to supply two large multimillion-dollar canneries.
Ua leai se ulu a ala. Schultz, 501. [Atu'u, Tutuila]

PAGE 45. *Left*, Religion plays an important role in American Samoa's life ... even on the assembly line. [Atu'u, Tutuila]
Middle, On Saturdays everyone in Samoa purchases, harvests, or catches the food for the Sunday feast.
"... they appeared very knowing merchants ..." Williams and Barff. [Fagatogo, Tutuila]
Right, Unlucky at fishing, a lavalava-clad youth catches his fish another way.
Ua tofo i tino matagi lelei. Schultz, 310. [Nu'uuli, Tutuila]

PAGE 46. With one of the most magnificent harbors in the South Seas, Pago Pago is a favorite port for ocean liners. [Fagatogo, Tutuila]

PAGE 47. *Left*, Disembarking passengers are welcomed with traditional Samoan songs and dances.
Ua iloa i va'a lelea. Schultz, 300. [Fagatogo, Tutuila]
Right, Situated on a harbor promontory, the Rainmaker Hotel, with its distinctive traditional architecture, provides hospitality and recreation for visitors to American Samoa.
Sa matou tu'u la'au mai nei. Schultz, 114. [Utulei, Tutuila]

PAGE 48. *Left*, A lavalava-clad youth makes an early morning deposit.
Ia 'oso 'ati'ati. Schultz, 504. [Fagatogo, Tutuila]
Right, The museum not only houses a fascinating permanent collection of Samoan artifacts but also exhibits local art and handicrafts.
Aua ne'i galo Afi'a i lona vao. Brown, 16. [Fagatogo, Tutuila]

PAGE 49. Through the Art Council of American Samoa, the museum sponsors programs that teach Samoa's youth such cultural skills as weaving, tapa making and carving.
E o'u le asō 'ae o oe taeao. Schultz, 423. [Fagatogo, Tutuila]

PAGE 50. *Top*, American Samoa's governor, lieutenant governor, legislature, and congressional delegate are all popularly elected.
"Men, women, and children ..." Williams. [Pago Pago, Tutuila]
Bottom, The legislature or *Fono* of American Samoa is bicameral. Senators are elected according to Samoan custom by the chiefs of each county. Members of the House of Representatives are popularly elected. [Fagatogo, Tutuila]

PAGE 51. The January opening ceremonies are always impressive. The *Fono* meets for two 45-day sessions each year. The second opening is in July.
"Upon the whole the government ..." Williams. [Fagatogo, Tutuila]

PAGE 52. American Samoa hosted the South Pacific Conference in 1982. The heads of state and government leaders of twenty-one island nations and territories met in Pago Pago to discuss matters of mutual interest and concern. [Tafuna, Tutuila]

PAGE 53. *Left*, The governor of American Samoa chaired the conference, which was conducted simultaneously in English and French.
Ua fuifui fa'atasi, 'ae vao 'ese'ese. Schultz, 91. [Utulei, Tutuila]
Top right, At the opening ceremonies, the Arts Council sang each of the twenty-one island groups anthems in its native tongue. [Pago Pago, Tutuila]
Bottom right, The head of every delegation is given a King's Kava. The drink is prepared outside the house rather than inside. A specially titled young man, *manaia*, wearing a *tuiga*, a headdress of bleached human hair decorated with feathers, beads, and shells, mixes the kava. The drink is strained through the fibers of the wild hibiscus.
Ua malie ma le faga i Pa'au. Schultz, 452. [Pago Pago, Tutuila]

PAGE 54. *Left*, When the new diocese of Pago Pago was formed, the Pope's special representative assisted the Samoan Cardinal. [Tafuna, Tutuila]
Right, The village of Leone, Tutuila, sent more than a hundred dancers to help Western Samoa celebrate the twenty-first anniversary of its independence. [Mulinu'u, Upolu]

PAGE 55. The Arts Council of American Samoa sent a delegation to the inauguration of the governor of Hawaii. [Honolulu, Hawaii]

PAGE 56. *Left*, Every four years the South Pacific Games are held. Attended by all the island nations and territories, they are the Olympics of the South Pacific. In 1983 American Samoa's team was one of the largest ever. [Apia Park, Upolu]
Right, American Samoa's volleyball team create an aerial wall. **O le ti'a ulu tonu lou finagalo.** Schultz, 245. [Apia Park, Upolu]

PAGE 57. One of American Samoa's boxers and the women's golf team are shown receiving their gold medals.
Top, **O le ua na fua mai Manu'a.** Brown, 49. [Vaivaseuta, Upolu]
Bottom, **E manatua pule, 'ae le manatua fa'alaeo.** Schultz, 518. [Matāutu, Upolu]

Milestones

We are all travellers through life and each culture creates its own particular milestones to mark human progress. These provide a rich and descriptive record that illustrate a people's values and cultural genius. To the usual milestones of birth, graduation, marriage, and death, Samoan culture has added the tattoo and the bestowal of a title. As the culture is oriented toward family and community, such social milestones as celebrating the arrival of the first missionary, a church dedication, and Flag Day have been included.

PAGE 58. When a baby is born, the father prepares and presents to the new mother a special drink made of warm coconut milk.
E tasi, 'ae afe. Schultz, 161. [LBJ Tropical Medical Center, Tutuila]

PAGE 59. *Left,* A boy's first haircut is marked by a gathering of the family's chiefs. A kava ceremony is held, and speeches made exhorting the boy to grow into an obedient youth, serving and sharing. After a prayer has been offered, the head of the family cuts the boy's hair.
E valavala a tumanu. Schultz, 397. [Leone, Tutuila]
Right, The lock of hair is woven into the family's headdress, and in this way the boy symbolically becomes a part of the family's ceremonial life. [Leone, Tutuila]

PAGE 60. *Top left,* At his high school graduation a young man touches his diploma to his head in a traditional gesture of appreciation and gratitude.
Ua tino le soifua ... Schultz, 428. [Mapusaga, Tutuila]
Bottom left, Young men are inducted into military service. Samoa contributes one of the highest percentages of any ethnic group to the U.S. armed forces.
Tau ina ta ma fa'apoi. Schultz, 351. [Utulei, Tutuila]
Bottom right, Laden with garlands of flowers and of shells from relatives and friends, the new inductees await their flight.
Ia manuia le malaga. Adage. [Tafuna, Tutuila]

PAGE 61. One of the finest international airports in the South Pacific connects American Samoa with the outside world. [Tafuna, Tutuila]

PAGE 62. Some of American Samoa's most educated young professionals assume the traditional marks of manhood. The tattoo, which extends from the upper pectoral muscles to below the knee cap, consists of twenty-two named elements. The tattoo master and his assistants work rapidly and efficiently. Six to eight sessions over a two-month period are ordinarily required to complete the traditional pattern.
E logo le tuli ona tātā. Schultz, 323. [Nu'uuli, Tutuila]

PAGE 63. *Left,* Traditionally the young women of the village encouraged the youths in their ordeal by singing during the operation. This young man has incorporated twentieth-century music and a headset.
E tupu le fafine fanau ... Kraemer p. 42. [Nu'uuli, Tutuila]
Middle, Several youths are always tattooed together, sharing one another's pain. At the conclusion of the operation, they present the tattoo master with flower leis and lengths of cloth. In symbolic recognition of their new status, he cracks an egg on each one's head. [Nu'uuli, Tutuila]
Right, After paying the tattoo master with fine mats and money, the newly tattooed youths and their host and hostess celebrate with a dance.
Ua maua le fili O Aumua le Sigano. Schultz, 417. [Nu'uuli, Tutuila]

PAGE 64. *Left,* Although a marriage is primarily to formalize and sanctify the relationship between the bride and groom, in Samoa it very much involves the extended families of each partner. The bride's relations contribute many fine mats and sleeping mats to the groom's family. These frequently run into hundreds if not thousands. [Fagatogo, Tutuila]
Right, It is incumbent on the groom's family to balance the exchange with money. [Fagatogo, Tutuila]

PAGE 65. The mats are redistributed among the groom's relatives, and the money to the bride's extended family, in proportion to the contribution made by each family member. The wedding exchange is between the families of the marriage partners. Although the material benefits do not go directly to the bride and groom, the exchange represents a major family undertaking orchestrated on their behalf.
Ua le sula fala o 'Ie'ie. Schultz, 267. [Fagatogo, Tutuila]

PAGE 66. *Top,* When a chief dies, the extended family chooses his or her successor. Unlike most Polynesian cultures, in Samoa a title is not inherited. Everyone related to the title has a chance to speak about the new candidate. Important considerations are age, wisdom, service to the family, and how close the connections are. Ideally, the new chief is chosen by consensus. Once chosen, he or she prepares for the *saofa'i,* an investiture or election feast. The *saofa'i* indicates the formal acceptance of the new *matai* by the village, county, and all of Samoa. [Leone, Tutuila]
Bottom, The extended family and village assemble to hear speeches exchanged by the talking chiefs.
O le vaivai o le fe'e. Schultz, 63. [Leone, Tutuila]

PAGE 67. *Left*, Each branch of the family presents the *matai* elect with symbolic food and the accoutrements of the new rank. [Leone, Tutuila]
Right, The men of the family prepare for the kava ceremony, where the new matai will be formally addressed by title for the first time. [Leone, Tutuila]

PAGE 68. The cost of the investure feast would astonish anyone not familiar with Samoan custom. A tremendous outlay of food and presentation of fine mats takes place between the extended family and the village. At this particular *saofaʻi*, 3,800 fine mats and $43,000 were redistributed.
Sāo faʻalālelei. Milner, 200. [Leone, Tutuila]

PAGE 69. *Left*, A carefull tally is kept of the contribution made by each branch of the family. Today, hand calculators and correction fluid make for more efficient record-keeping.
Avatu ni lo, aumai ni lo. Schultz, 58. [Leone, Tutuila]
Right, As each branch of the family makes its contribution, relatives sing and dance, encouraging the flow of fine mats. [Leone, Tutuila]

PAGE 70. *Top left*, As part of the custom, the family gives the chief of each contributing group a *sua* or special presentation consisting of a cooked pig, fowl, a coconut with one eye pierced, a dollar bill, taro cooked in banana or breadfruit leaves, a fine mat, and a *siapo* (tapa cloth), or length of fabric. These gifts symbolize the services rendered by the family — food, drink, money, and clothing.
"The Chief held one end of the cloth ..." Williams and Barff. [Leone, Tutuila]
Bottom left, Such large exchanges give relatives a chance to get together and discuss the latest news.
Ua lauiloa e pili ma sē. Schultz, 338. [Saʻilele, Tutuila]
Right. As a special mark of respect, not only the kava root but the whole bush is presented.
E sua le ʻava, ʻae to le ʻata. Schultz,196. [Saʻilele, Tutuila]

PAGE 71. *Left*, Kava is prepared and served to all chiefs present. [Leone, Tutuila]
Right, The highest talking chiefs of the village place their hands on the head of the *matai* elect to formally acknowledge the title and bless the new *matai*. [Leone, Tutuila]

PAGE 72. *Left*, With the acknowledgment of the family, elderly persons can have their funerals before they die. At their *lagi soifua*, they enjoy the speeches, feast, and fine mats given in their honor. [Pago Pago, Tutuila]
Right, All the branches of the family come and present fine mats and money. When the individual dies at some later date, a simple burial is performed with a small religious service. [Pago Pago, Tutuila]

PAGE 73. *Left*, The completion and formal opening of a new church is celebrated with a special church service and distribution of fine mats and food. Relatives of church members from all over the islands and even farther afield come to assist their families. [Aʻoloau, Tutuila]
Right, A *sua* is given to important guests and especially the carpenters who built the church.
O le mea a ʻOi. Brown, 32. [Aʻoloau, Tutuila]

PAGE 74. *Left*, Hundreds, if not thousands of fine mats are distributed.
Ia e vae o Vaeau. Schultz, 477. [Aʻoloau, Tutuila]
Right, Large kegs of salt beef are part of the distribution. The sociable Samoans, with their tight family organization, thoroughly enjoy such gatherings. Assistance is given freely as donors know that it will be returned on future occasions. [Aʻoloau, Tutuila]

PAGE 75. *Left*, Some older church women take time out to rest and enjoy a cool drink.
Sili le foe. Schultz, 87. [Faleniu, Tutuila]
Right, With their relatives, the young men of the congregation prepare a giant ground oven.
Tuai tuai ta te maʻona ai. Brown, 203. [Aʻoloau, Tutuila]

PAGE 76. *Left*, Everyone attending the celebration participates in the feast and is given a basket of food to take home and share with those unable to come.
Faʻatoetoe le muli o le ola. Schultz, 202. [Olosega]
Right, At night a dance is held to raise money for the new building. As a young girl of each family dances, relatives surround her and place money in her bodice or at her feet. [Faleniu, Tutuila]

PAGE 77. Off to the side, in the shadows, a small boy gives his own performance. [Faleniu, Tutuila]

PAGE 78. *Left*, In 1832, the Reverend John Williams of the London Missionary Society landed for the first time in what is now American Samoa. One hundred and fifty years later, the village of Leone and the whole Congregational Church celebrated the anniversary of his arrival and the formal introduction of Christianity. [Leone, Tutuila]
Right, The village choir sang several hymns and a solemn service was conducted. [Leone, Tutuila]

PAGE 79. Outside the church, the men of the village held a special kava ceremony in honor of the occasion.
"The name of the bay is Le One ..." Williams. [Leone, Tutuila]

PAGE 80. *Top left*, The annual celebration of Flag Day commemorates the cession of the islands to the United States. [Pago Pago, Tutuila]
Bottom left, All school children take part in the celebration.
O le taeao na i Saua. Brown, 8. [Pago Pago, Tutuila]
Middle, Villages vie with one another to produce the most spectacular mass dance.
Seʻi fono le paʻa ma ona vae. Brother Herman, 15. [Pago Pago, Tutuila]
Right, An interested spectator enjoys the proceedings. [Pago Pago, Tutuila]

PAGE 81. Village *fautasi* or longboats with crews of forty men or more compete.
O le vaʻa ua mafa tautai. Schultz, 276. [Off the coast]

Religion

Religion plays a very important part in Samoan culture. Most people go to church twice on Sunday and conclude each day with a family prayer. Children attend Pastor's school, youths enjoy Sunday evening Bible class, and adults attend choir practice several nights a week.

PAGE 82. Saturday is called *Aso To'ona'i*, the day when preparations are made for the Sunday feast. Before sunrise the young men of each family prepare ground ovens. At daybreak, first one puff of smoke, then another can be seen, until the whole valley floats in an early morning haze. Within fifteen minutes the trade winds disperse the smoke and one of the South Seas' most romantic sights is gone for another week. [South coast of Tutuila]

PAGE 83. *Left*, Dressed in white, a family makes its way to church. Each Sunday the road through the village is decorated with sprays of flowers.
O le gase a ala lalovao. Schultz, 195. [Vailoatai, Tutuila]
Right, Three churches within a mile underscore the importance of religion in Samoa. [Lepua/Aūa, Tutuila]

PAGE 84. *Left*, In Sunday school children learn Bible passages and hymns.
Ia uluulu matāfolau. Pratt, 37. [Nua, Tutuila]
Right, Morning service is over, and people go home for the Sunday feast or *to'ona'i*. [Taulaga, Swains Island]

PAGE 85. Although each family prepares its own *to'ona'i*, in many villages the Sunday meal is eaten communally. The pastor and chiefs eat together in one house and the untitled young men in another. Later, everyone relaxes for a Sunday rest. [Taulaga, Swains Island]

PAGE 86.*Left*, Many weddings are a beautiful blend of religion and culture. The bride and groom are seated on fine mats as the women of the family approach the altar with flower leis.
Ia fua le niu. Schultz, 178. [Fagatogo, Tutuila]
Right, The second Sunday in October, White Sunday or Children's Sunday, is the traditional day for baptisms. During the morning service, the small children recite Bible passages. In the afternoon the older children put on plays. This is a special day for recognizing children, a day when they receive new white clothes and the best of food. [Vailoatai, Tutuila]

PAGE 87. *Top*, The pastor and his wife hold school several afternoons a week. Many children learn to read and master the rudiments of arithmetic before beginning their formal education. [Fiti'uta, Ta'ū]
Bottom, On Sunday evening young people meet for Bible study and debates. On some weekends and holidays they play cricket and volleyball and on special occasions they exchange visits with the youth of other villages and islands.
O le uta a le poto e fetāla'i. Schultz, 507. [Taputimu, Tutuila]

PAGE 88. Choir members gather for practice several nights each week.
O le va'a fau pō fau ao. Schultz, 149. [Futiga, Tutuila]

PAGE 89. *Left*, In Manu'a, each family takes turn in providing the pastor with food. The men of the family get up at midnight and cook throughout the night. [Fiti'uta, Ta'ū]
Right, Before sunrise the baskets of food are delivered to the pastor's house.
Alofa moli pō. Schultz, 326. [Fiti'uta, Ta'ū]

PAGE 90. *Top*, When a death occurs, the village chiefs and untitled men assemble outside the house to pay their respects. The talking chiefs debate among themselves to determine who will address the family on behalf of the village.
O le pā ua sala i le maga. Schultz, 6. [Olosega]
Bottom, That night, various branches of the extended family pay their respects with speeches and fine mats. The village pastor and choir conduct a service and the women of the village sing hymns, staying with the family throughout the night. [Olosega]

PAGE 91. *Left*, In the morning, before the coffin is closed, everyone makes a last farewell. It is a time of intense emotion and grief.
Ua tagi le Fatu ma le 'Ele'ele. Brown, 153. [Olosega]
Right, Even in death the family stays close. The grave is dug and the funeral conducted on family land.
O le mamao a siu i tila. Brown, 93. [Fatumafuti, Tutuila]

Close of Day

There is a special ambience about the end of day in Samoa. Work is over in town and village. Men return from garden or sea, laden with food for the evening meal. This is the time for recreation and relaxation … On remote Swains, the lanterns are lit. All over American Samoa families gather for prayers before the evening meal. Farewell celebrations are held for guests who will depart the next day. A few families gather to discuss and plan for a forthcoming event. The stars come out. One by one the children fall asleep. The lights go out. The islands sleep.

PAGE 92. At the end of the day the food harvested is brought back to the village.
Māmā i avega si'i. Brown, 79. [Taputimu, Tutuila]

PAGE 93. High on the plateau, a young man finishes his work, climbs a palm and cuts down some branches. In minutes he weaves two baskets, fills them with breadfruit and taro, and slips them on a carrying stick. Following a switchback trail, he descends to his coastal village.
Ua pipili tia 'ae mamao ala. Schultz, 92. [Olosega]

PAGE 94. Assisted by his two sons, a father brings home the day's catch.
Ua tō i lologamata. Schultz, 68. [Leone, Tutuila]

PAGE 95. *Top,* The family gathers around its returning fisherman. The catch is handed over and the canoe bailed out and beached for the night. [Olosega]
Bottom, Spear fishermen walk on the reef with the day's catch (lobsters and fish.) [Le'alā, Tutuila]

PAGE 96. *Left,* Now there is time to relax and play. A smooth lava shelf becomes a slide.
Ua fa'ala'au tū i vanu. Schultz, 329. [Le'al'ā, Tutuila]
Right, A young man and a boy enjoy a game of marbles.
E mu'a le vao. Schultz, 350. [Ālao, Tutuila]

PAGE 97. *Left,* All around the islands, young people set up volleyball nets and everyone gets a chance to play.
Fa'ape'ape'a le tū. Schultz, 109. [Alofau, Tutuila]
Right, For some there's pleasure in just running.
Ua se i'a e sola. Schultz, 72. [Fogāgogo, Tutuila]

PAGE 98. *Top left,* Every season has its sport. From about June to December, village rugby teams compete for the championship.
Ua lelea le laumea. Pratt, 63. [Pago Pago, Tutuila]
Bottom left, Cricket is played from January to April. Each village chooses its own floral lavalava for a uniform and fields a competition team on Saturdays. Before the game, village chiefs and players pray. The chiefs encourage sportsmanship and exhort the young men to bring honor to their village.
Ua tusa tau'au. Schultz, 235. [Fūtiga, Tutuila]
Right, Almost every village has a cricket pitch. Ordinary games are quite informal and open to everyone, male and female alike. Each team's size is determined by how many people want to play. [Taputimu, Tutuila]

PAGE 99. *Left,* Championship matches involve village pride and draw sizeable crowds. [Faga'alu, Tutuila]
Middle, At the conclusion of each game the teams line up and shake hands. [Vailoatai, Tutuila]
Ua se vī e toli. Schultz, 218. [Vailoatai, Tutuila]
Right, American Samoa has produced some world-class football players. Each year, university and professional players return to share their expertise with Samoa's youth. This boy can't quite believe the size of the athlete's legs.
"Samoans are a fine race of people. The men …" Williams and Barff. [Leone, Tutuila]

PAGE 100. *Top left,* Even at night the fishing goes on. Traveling together the men leave in search of the elusive bonito. [Off the coast of Ta'ū]
Bottom, Once a year, in the middle of the night, the *palolo,* a small sea creature, rises from the reef to mate. It is a great delicacy. Thousands are scooped up in nets and emptied into pots held by women waiting on the beach.
O le upega e fili i le pō, 'ae talatala i le ao. Schultz, 24. [Lumā, Ta'ū]

PAGE 101. At sunset, the men go far beyond the reef — some twenty miles into the open sea. There at night, they shake coconut rattles in the water to make sounds like a wounded fish. Four lines of bait are put out. Sharks, attracted by the noise, circle the boat. One by one, the lines of bait are pulled in. The final line is drawn closer and closer. The men play with the shark the way a matador manipulates a bull. When the shark passes close enough, a fisherman slips a rope over its head. Tightening the noose, he presses down on the head and pulls up until the shark's mouth is wide open. His partner rams a pole down its throat and with five or six blows to the head, the shark is killed.
O le malie ma le tu'u. Brown, 101. [Out at sea]

PAGE 102. *Top left,* Every night on Swains, the lanterns are lit before the evening meal. [Taulaga, Swains Island]
Bottom left, All over American Samoa, families gather for evening prayers.
Talo lua Tuna ma Fata. Schultz, 385. [Taulaga, Swains Island]
Bottom right, On the eve of guests' departure, a farewell feast and celebration is held. [Taulaga, Swains Island]

PAGE 103. *Bottom left,* Children give an exuberant performance. [Village in Samoa]
Right, At times, their joy knows no bounds.
'Oa'oa i faleseu. Schultz, 102. [Village in Samoa]

PAGE 104. *Left,* At night, many families relax around their television.
Ua patipati ta'oto le Fe'epō. Schultz, 238. [Vailoauta, Tutuila]
Right, Up on Mt Alava, a lavalava-clad technician skilfully adjusts the channels. [Mt Alava, Tutuila]

PAGE 105. Through it all, the little ones sleep.
E tasi le pō 'ae ogaoga. Schultz, 484. [Taulaga, Swains Island]

PAGE 106. Late at night, an extended family discusses an impending celebration. Fine mats are gathered, kegs of salt beef stacked, and contributions made. [Sa'ilele, Tutuila]

PAGE 107. Beneath the Southern Cross, the passing night and new day meet on the horizon. A new cycle begins. [Pago Pago, Tutuila]

Epilogue